LIFE,
LIBERTY
AND THE
PURSUIT OF
SPEED

D0492732

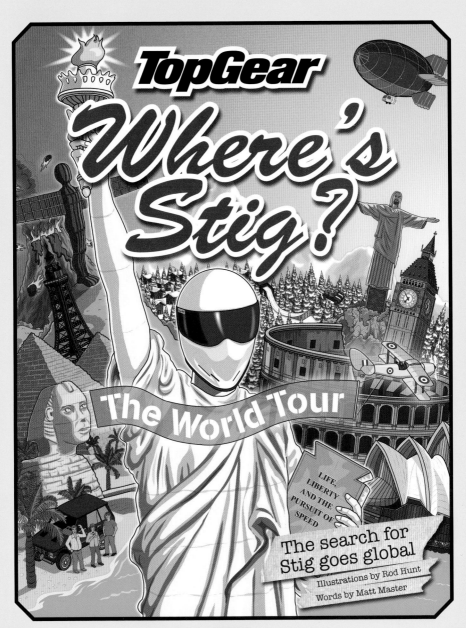

TopGear

Where's Stig?

The World Tour

LIFE,
LIBERTY
AND THE
PURSUIT OF
SPEED

The search for
Stig goes global

Illustrations by Rod Hunt

Words by Matt Master

BBC
BOOKS

Contents

WHAT TO FIND ON EVERY PAGE

The Stig

Jeremy

Richard

James

Morris Marina

Health &
Safety guy

BBC
accountant

Chairman,
Morris Marina
Owners Club

Stig's
vegetarian
cousin

Careless
Air advert

Cardboard
lav

The Great
Smell of Stig

Stig's
knee Lube

The Best of
Chas & Dave

Jeremy's
drum kit

Stig's
suitcase

Stig Earwax
Turkish Delight

Hammond's teeth
whitener

Voodoo Rubens
Barrichello

Introduction

While the pressures of global notoriety take their toll on lesser mortals, The Stig remains mysteriously unaffected. Maybe because it's only tyre pressures that ever trouble him. Maybe it's because he's not actually mortal.

Either way, as the gospel of *Top Gear* reaches ever farther around a world already slightly wary of three middle-aged men with bad hair and a penchant for wanton destruction, our monochrome motorhead keeps a watchful eye on his hapless chums.

Time to search them all out again, then. From the European hotspots of Monaco or Rome to the distant towers and jungles of the Americas, from the sun, sea, sand and, er, more sand of Australia, to the sun, sea, sand and slightly sticky pavements of Blackpool, the boys are making a very public mess of it. The Stig, meanwhile, is maintaining a typically low profile. Magnifying glasses at the ready…

London

Chaos reigns in the capital, and with 8 million lunatics running amok, three more aren't going to make much difference. But can The Stig find a suitably secretive vantage point?

The Alps

To the slopes, then, where
the dicey combination of ice,
altitude and thousand-foot drops
fails to register with our trio
of troublemakers. The Alps might
just be the ideal habitat for
a Stig though. Natural camouflage.
And no ducks.

New York

A quick visit to the land of excess, where petrol is free and Jeremy still looks comparatively thin. Stig's American cousin has just moved to the Big Apple too, and already eaten most of it.

Romania

Time for a change of pace: in Romania 'horsepower' is taken rather more literally and bio-fuel is what you get when you set fire to your goat. But this is the home of the world's greatest driving road. And Dracula. Stig is going to fit right in.

Down Under

You'd think there was little for Top Gear to ruin in the country that brought you Mad Max and shark attacks, but never underestimate the danger of three Poms with petrol in their blood, standing too close to the barbie.

Bolivia

If there's one place in the world where Top Gear shouldn't be able to make a nuisance of itself, it's the darkest depths of the Bolivian jungle. But that'd be reckoning without some of the most dangerous roads known to man and James May holding a machete.

Rome

Ah, Roma, epicentre of European art, religion and culture. Where better for the highbrow musings of Top Gear's world tour to find a spiritual home? With Minis at the ready and a cameo from Michael Caine, get ready for The Italian Bodge Job.

Caravan-Catraz

At long last a real chance for the boys to put their feet up: Top Gear loves a caravan. Ideally one that's on fire. Stig in the shadows, sausages at the ready, the emergency services on speed dial. And relax ...

Monaco

The highlight of the F1 calendar, Monaco is all about men flexing their plastic and girls who are mostly made of it. So the perfect place for a not-quite-human to blend seamlessly in, and for three pasty blokes with pot bellies to stand right out.

Rio de Janeiro

It's carnival time in Rio, the moment when thousands of girls in sparkly bikinis dance around in a rude way in front of a gigantic statue of Jesus. Sounds normal enough to us. Perhaps a bit too normal for Richard ...

Norway

Back to the frozen North, where Top Gear's own Winter Olympics is making a bit of a mess of the Norwegian countryside. Rocket-powered Minis, machine guns and yellow snow — this is Arctic survival without Bear Grylls.

Blackpool

Back home at last, and just in time to flick the switch in Blackpool. Stig is still nowhere to be seen, but can he seriously stay in hiding when Jeremy has his hands on the National Grid?

Checklist
Yet more stuff to try and find

London
- [ ] Austin Princess
- [ ] Boris Johnson
- [ ] Bulldog
- [ ] Guy Fawkes
- [ ] Guy Ritchie
- [ ] G-Whiz
- [ ] Mercedes Benz GL 500
- [ ] Pearly King & Queen
- [ ] Policeman & policewoman
- [ ] Quality Duck Houses
- [ ] Rover SD1
- [ ] Triumph Dolomite Sprint
- [ ] 2 litter pickers
- [ ] 2 punks
- [ ] 3 ducks
- [ ] 4 goths
- [ ] 5 congestion-charge signs
- [ ] 30 pigeons

The Alps
- [ ] BMW X5
- [ ] Ford Capri 2.8L
- [ ] Land Rover Freelander
- [ ] Man skiing in his underpants
- [ ] Nissan 300ZX
- [ ] Parachutist
- [ ] Porsche Cayenne
- [ ] Porsche 944
- [ ] Prince Charles
- [ ] Prince Harry
- [ ] Prince William
- [ ] VW Touareg
- [ ] Woman skiing wearing a bikini

New York
- [ ] Al Pacino
- [ ] Donald Trump
- [ ] Ford Mustang
- [ ] Girl holding a small white dog
- [ ] Girl in 'I ♥ NY' t-shirt
- [ ] Ice-cream seller
- [ ] Larsen's Biscuits advert
- [ ] London taxi
- [ ] Lou Reed
- [ ] Martin Scorsese
- [ ] Mayor Bloomberg
- [ ] Naked Cowboy
- [ ] Robert De Niro
- [ ] Standard Taxi Concept
- [ ] Stig's Fat American Cousin
- [ ] *Top Gear* America presenters
- [ ] Toyota Prius
- [ ] Waitress
- [ ] 6 cops in SWAT gear

Romania
- [ ] Alsatian dog
- [ ] Aston Martin DBS Volante
- [ ] Borat
- [ ] Cockerel
- [ ] Dacia Sandero
- [ ] Donkey
- [ ] Ferrari California
- [ ] GAZ Chaika
- [ ] Goat
- [ ] Lada Niva
- [ ] Lada Riva
- [ ] Lamborghini Gallardo Spyder
- [ ] Man carrying a sheep
- [ ] Moskvitch 408
- [ ] Romanian taxi
- [ ] Trabant
- [ ] Wartburg 353
- [ ] Woman carrying a man on her back
- [ ] Woman carrying a pig
- [ ] ZAZ 968
- [ ] 8 hens

Down Under
- [ ] AC/DC
- [ ] Baz Luhrmann
- [ ] Cate Blanchett
- [ ] Dame Edna Everage
- [ ] Eric Banner
- [ ] Ford Falcon XR6 Turbo Ute
- [ ] Ford GT Falcon Coupé
- [ ] Home-made Honda Prelude Ute
- [ ] Hugh Jackman
- [ ] Kylie Minogue
- [ ] Mark Webber
- [ ] Mad Max Interceptor
- [ ] Mel Gibson
- [ ] Mini
- [ ] Mini Moke
- [ ] Modern VW Beetle
- [ ] Nicole Kidman
- [ ] Nissan Navara Ute
- [ ] Proton Jumbuck Ute
- [ ] Russell Crowe
- [ ] Shane Warne
- [ ] Tattooed man
- [ ] Two-thumbs-up mullet man
- [ ] 4 koala bears
- [ ] 5 kangaroos
- [ ] 5 VW Campervans
- [ ] 9 BBQs
- [ ] 14 lifeguards

Bolivia
- [ ] Bolivian drummers
- [ ] Range Rover Classic
- [ ] Suzuki SJ
- [ ] Toyota FJ40 Landcruiser
- [ ] 5 llamas
- [ ] 5 moped riders
- [ ] 6 cyclists
- [ ] 7 capybaras

- ❏ 8 squirrel monkeys
- ❏ 28 roadside graves

Rome
- ❏ Alfa Romeo 8C
- ❏ Angel using a laptop
- ❏ Aston Martin DB4
- ❏ Golfing cardinal
- ❏ Lamborghini Gallardo
- ❏ Lamborghini Miura
- ❏ Lancia Beta
- ❏ Michael Caine
- ❏ Michelangelo's Stig
- ❏ Mona Lisa Stig
- ❏ Smart Car
- ❏ The Pope
- ❏ White Fiat 500 modern
- ❏ White Fiat 500 original
- ❏ Top Gear Polizia car
- ❏ 2 little devils

Caravan-Catraz
- ❏ Biohazard sign
- ❏ Dead bird
- ❏ Inflatable crocodile
- ❏ Kia Cerato
- ❏ Land Rover Discovery
- ❏ Man waving his walking stick
- ❏ Morris Minor
- ❏ 'No Fun' sign
- ❏ Poodle
- ❏ Spam
- ❏ Tractor
- ❏ Volvo 240
- ❏ VW Campervan
- ❏ Woman riding mobility scooter
- ❏ 2 children playing swingball

Monaco
- ❏ Anthony Hamilton
- ❏ Bernie Eccleston
- ❏ BMW Sauber
- ❏ Damon Hill
- ❏ Eddie Jordan
- ❏ Ferrari
- ❏ Force India
- ❏ Hispania racing team
- ❏ Jackie Stewart
- ❏ Jean Todt & Michelle Yeoh
- ❏ Jenson Button
- ❏ John Button
- ❏ La Rascasse
- ❏ Lotus
- ❏ Mark Webber
- ❏ Martin Brundle
- ❏ McLaren
- ❏ Mercedes GP
- ❏ Murray Walker
- ❏ Nigel Mansell
- ❏ Prince Albert
- ❏ Red Bull
- ❏ Renault
- ❏ Robert Kubica
- ❏ Ron Dennis
- ❏ Sebastian Vettel
- ❏ Torro Rosso
- ❏ Virgin Racing
- ❏ Williams

Rio de Janeiro
- ❏ Champagne waiter
- ❏ Clown
- ❏ Man wearing a white bandana with blue spots
- ❏ 2 photographers
- ❏ 3 women wearing top hats
- ❏ 5 footballs
- ❏ 7 Brazilian flags

Norway
- ❏ Audi Q7
- ❏ BMW X5
- ❏ Jaguar XK8
- ❏ Jay Kay
- ❏ Kevin McCloud
- ❏ Mitsubishi Evo World Rally Car
- ❏ Range Rover
- ❏ Red G-whiz
- ❏ Simon Cowell
- ❏ Suzuki Swifts
- ❏ Volvo XC90
- ❏ Skidoo
- ❏ Snowman
- ❏ Snow-woman
- ❏ 6 'No Caravan' signs

Blackpool
- ❏ Hammerhead Eagle i-Thrust
- ❏ Jaguar XJ
- ❏ Subaru Legacy
- ❏ VW Polo Blue Motion
- ❏ 4 people wearing paper crowns
- ❏ 5 bats
- ❏ 7 men dressed as Mexicans
- ❏ 7 men in Popeye suits
- ❏ 7 women with pink feather boas
- ❏ 8 green men
- ❏ 8 men dressed as Smurfs
- ❏ 8 men with angel wings & Indian headdresses
- ❏ 8 men with antlers
- ❏ 8 women in school uniform
- ❏ 8 women in pink hats
- ❏ 8 '117' men with funny moustaches
- ❏ 12 women with bunny ears

Acknowledgements

The publishers would like to thank Charlie Turner at Top Gear, Matt Master, and David and Yoko at Two Associates. Rod Hunt would like to thank Derek Brazell at The Association of Illustrators, Matt Thomas at Mosquito Music, Russell Cobb, Matthew Wood at Second Floor Studios & Arts & Lorna Russell and Caroline McArthur at BBC Books.

10 9 8 7 6 5 4 3 2 1

This format published in 2012 by BBC Books, an imprint of Ebury Publishing.
A Random House Group Company. First Published in 2010 as *Where's Stig: The World Tour.*

Text © Woodlands Books Ltd 2012
Artwork © Rod Hunt 2012

Top Gear (word marks and logos) is a trademark of the British Broadcasting Corporation and
used under license. Top Gear © 2005.

The Random House Group Limited Reg. No. 954009

Addresses for companies within the Random House Group can be found at
www.randomhouse.co.uk

A CIP catalogue record for this book is available from the British Library.

The Random House Group Limited supports The Forest Stewardship Council (FSC®), the
leading international forest certification organisation. Our books carrying the FSC label are
printed on FSC® certified paper. FSC is the only forest certification scheme endorsed by the
leading environmental organisations, including Greenpeace. Our paper procurement policy
can be found at www.randomhouse.co.uk/environment

ISBN 978 1 84 990563 3

Commissioning editor: Lorna Russell
Project editor: Caroline McArthur
Design: Two Associates
Production: Antony Heller
Printed and bound in Italy by Graphicom SRL